I0751485

BURNING BUSH
BOOKS

Who's Following You: Seven Strategies To Transform and Grow Your Influence

Adrienne Mayfield, Esq.

Who's Following You: Seven Strategies To Transform and Grow Your Influence

Published by Burning Bush Books

Copyright © 2021 by Adrienne Mayfield

All rights reserved

No part of this publication may be reproduced, stored in any retrieval system, or transmitted in any form, or by any means, mechanical, electronic, photocopying or otherwise without the prior written consent of the publisher, except as provided by United States of America copyright law.

First edition March 2021

For information about bulk purchases, please contact Adrienne Mayfield at amayfield2147@gmail.com.

Manufactured in the United States of America

ISBN: 978-0-9997694-7-8

All Scripture quotations, unless otherwise noted, taken from the Holy Bible, New King James Version.

Cover Design: Adrienne Mayfield

Cover Image: Desy Suryani

Visit the author's website at adriennemayfield.com

This book is dedicated to those who are being called from the cave . . . Show Yourself! It's your time!

Table of Contents

ACKNOWLEDGEMENTS

Thank you to everyone who has contributed to the maturation of all that I have become. Whether you prayed, rebuked, celebrated, hated, or challenged me, I appreciate you. It has taken all parts of my life and process to birth the leader you see today, so I am grateful for it all.

To those who have submitted to my leadership or been transformed by my teaching, I applaud you for staying the course. I count it a blessing and privilege to cover and birth gifts and help people grow and develop. Never forget that, "He who has begun a good work in you will finish it and bring it to completion."

FOREWORD

What exactly is influence? Is it the subtle ability to grow followers? Is it the skill necessary to convince people to emulate you? Or is it simply the leadership required to unite individuals under a common goal? I'd say that influence is even less than that. Influence is simply the ability to motivate and inspire. When taken from that vantage point, we discover that influence is really not difficult to obtain. The challenge actually lies in keeping the momentum going. This mystery drives our social media-crazed generation and also threatens to destroy creativity through comparison and competition.

To be a leader requires that someone actually be following you. If you are walking alone, touting the value of a thing, product, or a goal, and you cannot convince anyone that it is a noteworthy cause, you are not leading. Simply put, leaders must have someone to lead. There must be someone sold on what you're selling. There must be somebody buying what you're telling. Otherwise, you are just blowing smoke.

Over the next seven chapters, we will explore leadership from the perspective of Nehemiah, a leader who did not choose, fight, or lobby for leadership. He did not beg, lie, or cheat his way to the pinnacle of his tribe. He simply tapped into the principles of effective leadership and did what every good leader must be willing to do to be effective. He joined the fight, put his hands to work, and led.

If you truly want to gain a following, build influence, or garner support for a cause, you must understand the basic fabric from which true leaders are made. Join me and let's explore the issue. Be ready to take an honest assessment and really ask yourself, "Who's Following You?"

INTRODUCTION

Leonard Ravenhill, an evangelist and author, shared a story about something that occurred when American tourists visited Great Britain. The tourists encountered an old man sitting by a fence. They probed, "Were any great men born in this village?' The man confidently answered them, "Nope, only babies." This experience is a sobering reminder that we all start as just babies. What we become is largely dependent on who and what we allow to train us.

Therein is the rationale for writing this book. It is written for those called to lead and those who will submit to their leadership. Both must work together to create a symphony of agreement for success.

The biblical character, Nehemiah faced many of the challenges that confront every leader. He was born at a very difficult time for his nation. They were enslaved and displaced. They had returned to Jerusalem but were immobilized by their defeat. In short, they lost their identity. They forgot who they were called to be. This is the backdrop of the people Nehemiah is called to lead.

This backdrop reminds us that leading is not always easy. It requires determination and "stick-with-it-ness." Not everyone who needs your leadership will even know they need you, and many will be so stuck that they will fight you every step of the way. Still, who God has called you to be is inescapable. Even if you think you can outrun your destiny for a season or if challenges subvert the process, ultimately, your calling will scream so loudly that it cannot be ignored.

In my own life, I have tried many times to hide in the background. I've tried to blend in and project responsibility on others around me. I was largely unsuccessful at blending in. Even when I didn't want to lead, even when I pushed people away, they kept coming to find me—in restaurants, in malls, in dressing rooms, in restaurant bathrooms literally everywhere. Finally, I embraced it. I accepted my fate. I am called to lead.

Perhaps you have also tried to escape or run from your leadership potential. Let me save you a lot of time and energy. There is no running or escaping it. If you don't want to accept my word, you can also check with Jonah. Some way, somehow, the Sovereign God of the universe will recover the investment he has put inside of you. So, you may as well get about the business of cultivating and developing the gift inside of you. Work on mastering the skill of managing people, processes, and systems so that you can lead. Focus on streamlining the sound of your voice so you can glance behind you, survey your legacy, and know with certainty just "Who's Following You."

CHAPTER 1

CREATE FROM YOUR PASSION

Many people begin their journey to build influence and following all wrong. They focus their strategy on what everyone else is already doing, what the common trends are, or what social media gurus say. Though information is power, that information does nothing if you have not discovered the "why" behind your desire to build a following. You must identify why you are called before you beginning planning what you should do next.

You cannot make people follow you. They must choose to. Therefore, you must focus on revealing your value. You have to convince them that you possess something they actually want or need. You must project the confidence and assurance that you are leading them somewhere. It is impossible to do that if you, yourself, have not identified the why behind your what.

Jumping in full throttle can end in burnout if you do not discover the reason behind your drive. It is imperative that you identify your assignment. For what reason were you born? Why are you in the Earth? To assist in answering these questions, you must discover:

Why do I want to gain a following?

What is driving me?

Is this the thing that keeps me awake at night?

Would I do this for free if no one ever knew I was doing it?

Is this tied to my calling and the reason why I was born?

The answers to these questions give you a clue and direction to something sustainable. Identifying your why provides motivation and excitement.

You will know that you are on the right track when you are more driven by the people you are called to serve than your own fame or influence. Understanding your call to serve will keep your focus on the needs of those you serve rather than yourself. When you focus more on meeting needs and establishing yourself as a resource, you become someone whose very presence and value cannot be ignored.

When the Israelites come out of Babylon, Nehemiah does not return to Jerusalem. He is in Persia serving the king. He has obtained a position of influence. Nehemiah is the cupbearer. Being the cupbearer is a position of trust and loyalty. It is his responsibility to test the integrity of everything the king eats and drinks. He must inspect everything first. Think Secret Service on a whole other level.

Even though Nehemiah is separated from his people, he never forgets them. His commitment and devotion will become even clearer as we walk through his leadership journey.

One day, Nehemiah's brother comes to see him. Nehemiah immediately inquires about the welfare of his people. This is the true heart of being a leader and building a following. You must have a heart for those you are called to lead. The desire to lead must be sourced by your passion for helping others, not from the notoriety or platform you wish to achieve.

People recognize fakes. And they don't like them. If you are someone who is using people as a means to an end, you will not last. Your self-centered approach may last for a while, but it will not sustain you for the long haul. When people discover your true motivation, they will be turned off, and the "following" you gained will begin to disappear into thin air. People appreciate and respect authenticity and everyone wants to know they matter. Never forget that. Make your motivation for leading be the people you serve and help and not your own selfish ambition. This is the key to longevity.

Nehemiah receives a word that his people need help. They are in great distress. More specifically, Nehemiah 1:3 reveals that the messengers tell him, "The wall of Jerusalem is also broken down, and its gates are burned with fire." Broken walls are breaches of protection and burned gates block the freedom to exit. They also prevent entry. None of this is good. To further drive the point home, they tell Nehemiah that the people have become a reproach!

Nehemiah's response is swift and decisive. He knows how to get the answers he seeks for his problem. He weeps, mourns, fasts, and prays. He knows and understands that something has to be done. Still, he doesn't just launch out and start doing anything.

The need is obvious, but Nehemiah makes no assumptions about the next steps. He immediately seeks the God of the universe for answers and solutions.

This is the key to your success. To accomplish anything impactful in this world requires something greater and more powerful than you. That something is actually not a thing. He is God. It would be foolish for someone to embark on a building project with knowledge of an existing blueprint but refuse to use it. This is the futility of seeking to build a following, or anything else for that matter, without the incomparable, immutable, intel of God. He knows everything, so anyone wise learns and accepts that He must be consulted.

I have just finished reading a story about a young woman, 18 years old, with over 1.4 million followers. She just committed suicide. In the last month, several well-known "influencers" have died or committed suicide. Let this sober you. To build a following that is not connected to the proper foundation can be fatal.

God wants us to flourish and prosper. This is His heart. If you endeavor to give Him honor with your gifts and talents, He will support you in the process. He will help you help people. He will give you a winning strategy. He will help you win. As long as you are following Him, He will help you build a following that ultimately points to Him. To some of you, this may sound too deep or spiritual. You might be thinking, but my industry isn't church or religion. Why would God help me with this? You must remember—God is the Creator of EVERYTHING! Colossians 1:16 tells us, "For by Him all things were created that are in heaven and that are on earth, visible and invisible, whether thrones or dominions or principalities or powers. All things were created through Him and for Him." You never have to wonder if God is concerned about something He has called you to lead or build. He is involved in ALL things!

If you have made the mistake of trying to build on your own or build for selfish motives, it's not too late. You can begin again. Approach God as Nehemiah did, tell Him you are sorry that you left Him out. Acknowledge His Sovereignty. Thank Him for hearing you. Then tell Him you have tried to build without Him. Nehemiah's prayer in Chapter 1:5-11 gives a great blueprint.

> And I said: 'I pray, Lord God of heaven, O great and awesome God, You who keep Your covenant and mercy with those who love You and observe Your commandments, please let Your ear be attentive and Your eyes open, that You may hear the prayer of Your servant which I pray before You now, day and night, for the children of Israel Your servants, and confess the sins of the children of Israel which we have sinned against You. Both my father's house and I have sinned. We have acted very corruptly against You and have not kept the commandments, the statutes, nor the ordinances which You commanded Your servant Moses. Remember, I pray, the word that You commanded Your servant, Moses, saying, 'If you are unfaithful, I will scatter you among the nations; but if you return to Me, and keep My commandments and do them, though some of you were cast out to the farthest part of the heavens, yet I will

> gather them from there, and bring them to the place which I have chosen as a dwelling for My name.' Now these are Your servants and Your people, whom You have redeemed by Your great power, and by Your strong hand. O Lord, I pray, please let Your ear be attentive to the prayer of Your servant, and to the prayer of Your servants who desire to fear Your name; and let Your servant prosper this day, I pray, and grant him mercy in the sight of this man." For I was the king's cupbearer."

Nehemiah confesses the things they have been guilty of that could block God from justly blessing them. Then he reminds God of His covenant and promise to bless them and asks that God hear his prayer. This is both wisdom and preparation. As we will see, Nehemiah knows that to even begin to assist, he has an insurmountable challenge ahead. To rescue his people, he will have to be released from his current assignment as cupbearer to the king.

CHAPTER 2

GATHER YOUR RESOURCES

Creating influence cannot be just for the moment. It has to be bigger than that to ensure that your passion does not fizzle. Creating influence must be about legacy and creating a path for others to follow. Influence for influence's sake does little of lasting value. The focus of influence should be to impact generations and create a ripple effect that introduces something powerful in the Earth. This can only be achieved when the leader is willing to make sacrifices and utilize their influence for the good of those that follow.

Nehemiah enjoys a position of great importance and prominence, and his love for the people remains. But, he is confronted with a conundrum. He feels a pull toward his destiny. He wants to help rebuild the city, but he can't just leave. He is one of the top officials to the king. As cupbearer to the king, Nehemiah is responsible for ensuring the safety of the wine before the king drinks it. He often drinks first to ensure that it is not harmful or poisonous. His position is no light thing. To be entrusted in this way means Nehemiah's presence is invaluable.

Nehemiah cannot just casually approach the king and ask for a day off. His is not like our modern culture. His position isn't one he can just call in sick from or be covered for by a friend. His position is one of superior importance; the king's very life depends on his integrity and presence.

This position was part of God's plan in teaching Nehemiah to cultivate qualities that must be present in a leader. Leaders must be trustworthy, stable, and dependable. Many times, we question our journey and don't understand how our current lot will get us to our desired goal. Do not despair. Mistakes or bad experiences do not possess the ability to circumvent God's plan. Even a position that we might consider insignificant can provide the very training we need for our future. With God, nothing is wasted.

As time passes, the anguish of Nehemiah's heart begins to show in his countenance. His people are scattered and broken. He is despondent. What makes you sad? What issue or problem keeps you up at night? What is breaking people around you that breaks your heart? The answers to these questions give clues to the areas where you will be most effective. They point you to the people you are called to lead.

Approximately four months pass, and one day the king has a question for Nehemiah. He asks him why his face is sad. You are probably thinking, "What's the big deal about that?" It is more than a big deal. Cupbearers were never supposed to show emotion as they served the king. Breaking this rule could mean they were sentenced to death! Remember, though, that Nehemiah has been praying and fasting. Nehemiah responds, "May the king live forever. Why should my face not be sad when the city, the place of my father's tombs lies in waste, and its gates are burned with fire?" Nehemiah 2:3.

When the king asks Nehemiah what he wants, Nehemiah prays to God and makes his request. "If it pleases the king, and if your servant has found favor in your sight, I ask that you send me to Judah, to the city of my father's tombs that I may rebuild it." After receiving an affirmative answer and setting a time, Nehemiah asks for letters of permission and letters for timber. Why not? When Nehemiah discerns that he has the king's favor, he makes requests for everything he needs.

Building requires boldness. You must be willing to ask for whatever you want, whether it is a loan from a bank or to rent or buy a building. Ask God for favor and then be bold. Consider your needs and don't be afraid to seek assistance to acquire your resources. Proverbs 21:1 tells us, "The king's heart is in the hand of the Lord, Like the rivers of water; He turns it wherever He wishes." Once you get God's approval, favor and doors will open.

Nehemiah asks for a letter so that he can pass through safely. This is synonymous with someone using their influence to make certain that the plan they are building will succeed. Building as a leader requires focus and establishing connections with like-minded individuals who can resource and supply the vision. As you build, you should seek financiers and individuals who will help you bring your vision to fruition.

News spreads that Nehemiah is on his way to seek the welfare of his people. When word reaches Sanballat and Tobiah, Nehemiah 2:10 tells us that they "were deeply disturbed that a man had come to seek the well-being of the children of Israel."

Their displeasure tells us what we need to know to label them as friend or foe, but we will leave them for now. Recognize the existence of your opposition but don't lose focus. Just keep going.

CHAPTER 3

COUNT THE COST OF BUILDING

When Nehemiah arrives in Jerusalem, he does something interesting. Before making any decisions, calling a press conference, or scheduling a Rebuilding Live, he simply looks around. He takes three whole days to survey the scene. Patience seems to be a challenge for most builders in our microwave society. Planning in secret takes real discipline, but it's really a good idea.

This aspect of leadership addresses planning and building vision. Nehemiah surveys the task ahead and counts the cost. As a leader who wishes to build a following, you must survey the needs of those you are called to, develop systems and processes to address their needs, and ensure the resources are in place for the long haul. In the course of building, it is imperative that you begin to gather support for the cause. To accomplish this, you must be able to show your commitment to the journey for those you lead.

When you roll out a new product or idea, plan well. Take time to think through your ideas and perhaps bounce them off a trusted confidante. No one wants to join an unorganized anything! Take assessment, evaluate, then pitch the idea. Plan your launch, your idea, your website, your course, or your team project. Don't just be haphazard or lackadaisical. Remember, you only get one chance to make a first impression. Ensure that your "great reveal" is clear, concise, and well-done. Make certain that you give clear directions that people can follow.

After assessing the area, Nehemiah takes three men with him to check things out. Then, Nehemiah shares the harsh truth with the people. "You see the distress that we are in, how Jerusalem lies in waste, and its gates are burned with fire." Nehemiah 2:17. There is no denying it. The state of their city is in ruins.

As a leader, you must be willing to tell the truth. Making people feel comfortable can be detrimental to their growth. Until there is recognition of a problem, there is no desire to change. Sometimes, leaders lie or manipulate the truth to gain or maintain a following. This is a huge mistake. Know that the people who are drawn to you are your responsibility. You must steward them well. You are called to move them to change and development, not their comfort.

Nehemiah pitches the idea as a joint venture. He is not asking them to do anything that he is not willing to do. Effective leaders prove devotion to their followers by joining them in the process. Partnership requires a level of transparency but not translucency. To allow those you lead to see some parts of your humanity builds trust and community. Still, you must be careful. The world of social media, for many, gives the illusion of authentic relationship. Build with connection but keep your private life as your own.

Nehemiah implores the people to join him in his quest to build so that others will not look poorly on them. He says, "Come let us build the wall of Jerusalem that way we may no longer be a reproach." Nehemiah 2:17. Nehemiah uses our innate human desire to be revered and respected to his advantage. As you establish a following, keep this fact at the forefront of your mind. Everyone desires acceptance and appreciation, and everyone wants to be better. It is your job to help your followers discover what "better" is and help them develop a plan and strategy to get there.

Nehemiah's strategy is successful. The people respond in the affirmative. "So they said, "Let us rise up and build." Then they set their hands to this good work." Nehemiah 2:18.

Whatever your industry, your goal should be to build leaders. You must endeavor to build trailblazers who can face challenges, meet their problems head-on, and win! Many of those you serve may not see themselves as leaders. They will come to you with different stories and experiences. Teach them to use their stories as passports. Direct them to use their life experience to gain access to their destiny. As you do, you will find that you are not only building a business; you are building people. Whenever you build people, the payoff is huge.

As Nehemiah is rallying his troops for rebuilding, Sanballat and Tobiah appear on the scene again. In Chapter Two, we learned that they were "deeply disturbed" to discover that Nehemiah comes to assist the children of Israel. As Nehemiah grows support for his cause, Sanballat and Tobiah realize they need to do something to stop the work before it begins. "They laughed at us, and despised us, and said, 'What is this thing you are doing? Will you rebel against the king?" Nehemiah 2:19.

Nehemiah gives them a very pointed and direct response, "The God of heaven Himself will prosper us. Therefore, we His servants will arise and build, but YOU [emphasis added] have no heritage or right or memorial in Jerusalem." Nehemiah 2:20. Basically, Nehemiah tells them, Look dudes, God is on our side. He is helping us. We are doing this whether you like it or not. Do I need to remind you that this belongs to us? It has nothing to do with you. Mind your business. Nehemiah wasn't playing and you can't either. If you allow naysayers to distract you, you may never realize your destiny. Resolve to push past detractors and fight for your goals. This is true leadership.

Preparing for adversity is wise as there will always be opposition to any forward momentum. Perhaps you are experiencing this fact first hand. Maybe you have started to build and found that your support system is lacking. Maybe you built with people who have betrayed you or walked away. That is an inevitable part of doing anything great. Leading requires resilience, strength, and very thick skin. You cannot stop building just because some things don't go as planned. You must maintain your resolve.

CHAPTER 4

BUILD A WINNING SQUAD

Building a following means you must first learn how to build a team. An effective team is comprised of strong individuals who supplement your weaknesses and complement your strengths. Deal with any part of your personality that is driven by an obsession with competition and comparison. Often leaders will make the mistake of surrounding themselves with clones or groupies. Both are a hindrance to your growth as a leader. It will stifle the development of your team.

Often clones have the same strengths as you. They are so similar that they may not add any diversity or value to the team. Groupies are individuals who are so enamored by you that they will serve little purpose when you need a sounding board or a nudge in another direction. Don't be afraid to surround yourself with strong people or strong personalities. Only an insecure leader is afraid of engaging competent people. Be honest with yourself about your weaknesses, then staff your strengths. Diversity is a good thing, especially when establishing a team.

Keep in mind that it is your responsibility to create a team that will make your life easier. The less you have to be hands-on provides more time for content creation, vision casting, and wealth acquisition. Focus your energy on unifying the team around a common goal. As you delegate responsibility, the team will begin to grow in their confidence and aptitude. People tend to be more dedicated when they actually can contribute in a meaningful way. When an issue or a problem arises, resist the temptation to always come to the rescue. Allow the pressure to rise until someone steps up. Build leaders as you lead!

Everything works better when you have the right squad. There's a popular saying that is actually quite instructive, "If you want to know your future, look at your five closest friends." No truer statement has been said! To be an effective leader, you have to surround yourself with the right people. Establish a team that includes team members for planning and strategy and some for execution. Everything becomes easier if you staff yourself appropriately. No man is an island and no one person can do everything. You will find yourself quickly burning out if you do not set processes in place that assign tasks to other gifted individuals. Value talent in others; do not resent it, and you will discover that it can work for you. Surround yourself with everything that you lack, and you will never suffer for anything. Nothing shall be missing, nothing broken.

In order to build a successful team, you must staff yourself with leaders, not just followers. This is a mistake that many leaders make. Because of insecurity and fear, they try to locate team members who are weaker in character, skill, and strength.

THIS IS A MISTAKE. The goal of a true leader is replication in the Earth. It does no good for you to have to be present for every decision, at every meeting, or in every minute decision.

Staffing your squad with leaders guarantees that you can train them to train others in your philosophy and organizational structure. That frees you to do what you do best, whether administrating, creating, leading, or building. If you are inundated with all the required tasks that make your engine run, you will crash and burn.

It is important to be a leader that assists followers in answering their own questions. As you grow people, encourage them to be parties in their own growth and success. As you teach skills or strategies, each one should reach one. This is the real way to see your impact and influence grow. When people have no investment in something, its value decreases. Make sure you require individuals to invest in their own success and growth; otherwise, they will always be dependent on you, and as we covered earlier, burnout will be the natural result.

Leading with strength demands that you are supported by other strong leaders. They become a stabilizing force. They help you see through your blind spots and provide support for the building process. Without the support of strong individuals, you will quickly find yourself exhausted. It can be challenging to place your dream into the hands of another, but the time that sharing the load makes available cannot be emphasized enough.

As you begin to grow and build, you will find that the additional time and space will provide clarity and refreshment.

You might also discover that new ideas begin to flow more readily as well.

CHAPTER 5

STAND THROUGH TESTING

Having a strong support system is even more important as you become more successful. Success brings many trappings that promise enjoyment, lifestyle enhancement and fun, but success also attracts competition, criticism, and detractors. If you do not have a plan in place for how you will deal with this reality, when opposition or difficulty show up, you might be immobilized. I'm in no way suggesting that you embrace the saying, "Let your haters be your motivators," but I am simply giving you a warning and sound advice. Not everyone will celebrate your growth. Everything won't go according to plan. If you do not acknowledge and make plans to overcome this reality, the hit to your esteem could set you back for months or even years. In the case of some, the pressure of criticism and setbacks forces them to abort building altogether.

There will be some who will click like, follow, and share. They will celebrate your success and be genuinely happy for you. They will offer support, provide financial resources, and lend their hands to the project. Then there will be others who watch from afar, simply observing, waiting to see if you will succeed or fail. If you persevere and make it, they may join you. If you fail, you may never know they were watching at all. Still, there are others who will secretly or overtly wish for your demise. The last group, though, are the ones you might want to take note of.

You don't need to stop the work or place too much of your focus on them, but to ignore their existence would be foolish. Identify disloyal and inconsistent associates early on, so you don't mistake them as integral people for your team. If you have already experienced this issue or are facing it right now, do not despair. Jesus completed his mission with Judas right by his side. He walked with him, shared dinner with him, and allowed him to be a part of his circle even though he knew he would betray him. Jesus's model teaches us that we can overcome betrayal and still flourish. Leaders may bow, but they do not break!

It is a good thing that Nehemiah staffs his team well because Sanballat and Tobiah aren't done. They return to try to subvert the work again. "But it so happened when Sanballat heard that we were building the wall, that he was furious and very indignant and mocked the Jews." Isn't it empowering to know that you are not the only one who has not been fully supported in your dreams? Aren't you comforted to know that you are not the first person to face opposition? Doesn't it feel reassuring to know that you can keep going even when everyone isn't backing your cause? I remind you again that even though everyone will not be excited when you decide to build, build anyway.

Persecution and opposition reveal the weak spots in your plan and team. They also help everyone maintain focus. Most importantly, obstacles keep our eyes fixed on the one who makes everything work. Without His support, everything falls flat on its head anyway. Psalms 127:1 reminds us, "Unless the Lord builds a house, those who build it labor in vain. Unless the Lord watches over the city, the watchmen stay awake in vain." We must depend on God for every stage of our growth as leaders. Whether you have one follower, ten, or ten thousand, your longevity is dependent on acknowledging God as the Supreme Ruler of Everything. Every opposition that comes against you comes against Him.

Don't put your focus on fighting people. The battle is not about defeating people. Ephesians 6:12 reminds us, "For we do not wrestle against flesh and blood, but against principalities, against powers, against the rulers of the darkness of this age, against spiritual hosts of wickedness in the heavenly places." Ultimately it is the enemy of our souls who tries to block our success and destiny; men are simply the tools he uses for his purposes. Maintain laser-sharp focus and don't be deterred or distracted. Make a decision right now to be stand tall and strong and remain unbothered.

People will doubt you, say you're crazy, and tell you it won't work. Build anyway. Let nothing and no one take you out of your game. It is yours to run. Plan and execute. Leave all the fighting to God. If He has given you a dream or vision, and you have dedicated it to Him, He will back it. That's all you need to know to trust that it will work. Do not attempt to build anything without God. Partner with Him. Plan with Him. He will help you build an impenetrable plan. Romans 8:31 assures us, "If God be for us, who can be against us?" You plus God equals the majority.

As the work continues, Sanballat and Tobiah are angered even more. They begin to conspire to attack the Israelites and confuse their work. The enemies' persistence teaches leaders that though we must not be ignorant of the enemy's devices, we don't focus our energy on plans to stop us. We don't stop building because someone threatens to "cancel" us, drop a project, or try to start a social media war. We simply use opposition and setbacks to remind us that we must guard and protect our dream, surrounding it with planning and prayer.

The most important thing to remember as you lead and build is that God is actually doing the work if you have chosen to serve him. We should not attempt to build a system, a business, a relationship or anything else without God. Wisdom demands that we consult Him each step of the way. The moment we go rogue and do things on our own, things will fall. God desires to partner with us. You don't have to build alone.

Plan for opposition but don't stop building. Deal with fear and crush it on its head. Do not entertain fear of failure or lack. Establish processes that are failproof, but accept that things will happen that you could not have anticipated or planned for. When these mishaps occur, you can remain stable if you dedicated your plan to God, staffed your weaknesses, and established processes and systems.

CHAPTER 6

MASTER THE ART OF PSYCHOLOGY

When Nehemiah faces opposition, he doesn't stop, but he put a plan in place. He develops a specific strategy. "So it was, from that time on, that half of my servants worked on construction, while the other half held the spears, the shields, the bows, and wore armor. . . . Every one of the builders had his sword girded at his side as he built." Nehemiah 4:16, 18. Half build and half protect. This is a militarized strategy that protects the integrity of what you are building.

Employing this strategy can, at times, be tricky and it is definitely something that is often neglected. You must build and war for your dreams. You don't get to choose which you will do. Both must occur simultaneously. The moment you stop building, the enemy will try to destroy your work. The moment you stop fighting, you will not have the protection and foresight to build. You might be tempted to remove your focus from warring or building. But I am telling you from experience that this decision is a mistake. You will lose productivity by using all your resources for building if no one is watching and protecting the future of what you are building.

It would serve you well to take time to understand how people think. Understanding people will help you avoid disappointment and heartbreak. As you build your legacy, there will be casualties. There will be some people who begin the work that drop off after time. Sometimes there will be opposition that comes from within. Wherever there are people, there is the likelihood of conflict.

Such is the case with Nehemiah. The wall project is moving along. He has averted the crisis of Sanballat and Tobiah. But now, he is faced with conflict among the people he leads. The people complain because some have been taking advantage of each other. More specifically, they say, "Yet now, our flesh is the flesh of our brethren, our children are their children, and indeed we are forcing our sons and our daughters to be slaves and some of our daughters have been brought into slavery. It is not in our power to redeem them, for other men have our lands and vineyards." Despite having been previously enslaved themselves, the richer Jews are exacting usury against their own people, sometimes taking children as slaves for payment! Can you imagine! The greed of the people infuriates Nehemiah. How could they repeat the same behavior as had been done to them? Yet such is human nature.

Often as we build, we experience infighting within the team. Competition arises. People lobby for positions, and backbiting and sabotage sometimes occur. Worse yet, people sometimes negotiate side deals and use resources for their personal gain. Do not despair. The Bible reminds us, "What has been done will be again, what has been done will be done again, there is nothing new under the sun." Ecclesiastes 1:9. People are people, and many cannot resist the temptation of greed and impropriety. Don't take it personally. Embrace the opportunity to handle difficulties and challenges with grace as they purify and strengthen your aptitude to lead. You are built for this! Take the licking, but keep right on ticking!

Take note of Nehemiah's response. "After serious thought, I rebuked the nobles and rulers and said to them, each of you is exacting usury from his brother. So, I called a great assembly." Nehemiah doesn't toy around with them. He is well aware of the end result of confusion and chaos. He calls a meeting and tells them they must restore all. If as you lead, you sense or learn that there is trouble brewing, don't ignore it. Don't hope it will go away. Grab the bull by the horns and address it directly. Call a meeting. Set a timetable. Squash it before it grows. Dissension is like cancer. Kill it before it spreads. A quick response can save your organization, project, or community from disaster.

The primary skill a leader must perfect is people management. You cannot be afraid to deal with conflict. You must be firm and decisive. You must be integral and committed. You must be resilient and strong. You must be determined, focused, and dependable. You must demonstrate by your example what it means to sacrifice for the good of the people you lead. They must view you as someone like them, but yet one they respect and find worthy of emulation. Many of those you are called to lead and serve will likely have been wounded by former leaders. They can sense fake, abusive, opportunists a mile away. Be different.

Nehemiah offers an example for this issue as well. After he rebukes the people, he reminds them that he has led by example. Though he could have taken the governor's provisions, he refuses pillaging his brothers. Even though he had opportunities to take advantage of things, he refused.

> Moreover, from the time I was appointed to be their governor; twelve years, neither I nor my brothers ate the governor's provisions. But the former governors who were before me laid burdens on the people and took from them bread and wine, besides forty shekels of silver. Yes, even their servants bore rule over the people, but I did not do so because of the fear of God. Nehemiah 5:14-15

Previous governors had taken from the people and added to their burden, but Nehemiah refused. He joins the people in the work and does not ask to be given governor provisions.

> Now that which was prepared daily was one ox and choice sheep. Also, fowl were prepared for me, and once every ten days, an abundance of all kinds of wine. Yet in spite of this, I did not demand the governor's provision because the bondage was heavy on these people." Nehemiah 5:18

How different you will be if you employ this principle. If you do not take from the people but seek to offer them value and offer give yourself as a resource, you will be sought out like a precious jewel.

Perhaps you have survived attacks, resets, redos, and betrayal. Some ideas have worked; some failed; other lessons cost you thousands to learn.

If you are still standing, you might be tempted to stop to celebrate your victories or catch a breath. Be careful. If you have staffed yourself properly, you may be able to afford to rest for a moment, but you still have to keep your eyes on the goal. The enemy seeks an opportunity to attack when we celebrate and when we mourn. The lesson here is to remain vigilant and focused. If you have accomplished your goals, plan for the next phase. Solidify the foundations. Check for cracks. Examine your team. Determine whether everyone should be part of the next phase. If you don't evaluate your systems, strategy, and staff along the way, you could be caught off-guard. Success attracts followers. Both Good and Bad.

You must guard yourself. Be careful as you ascend in prominence and influence. Make sure that you do not use people as pawns or manipulate them for your own selfish gain. If you are predatory as a leader, you will produce a culture that replicates that character. As the leader goes, so goes the organization.

We are still tracking with Nehemiah, right? We are still learning from his challenges and difficulties in building.

> Now it happened when Sanballat and Tobiah, Geshem, the Arab, and the rest of our enemies heard that I had rebuilt the wall and that there were no breaks left in it, that Sanballat and Geshem sent to me saying, "Come let us meet together among the villages in the plain of Ono." Nehemiah 6:2

You guessed it! Sanballat and Tobiah have not given up. They are determined to stop the work, but since their strategies have not been unsuccessful, so they shift their gaze to the man leading the work.

Everyone knows that to destroy a movement, you focus on the leader. If the leader is removed, the work will stop as those who follow may be paralyzed or demoralized to quit. We have seen it happen all throughout history.

One example most will be familiar with is Dr. Martin Luther King, Jr. He led a nonviolent movement to obtain equal rights. The movement grew; his influence grew. People followed him and began to accept his belief that all men really could be equal. To stop the movement, the enemy took the head of the leader. In Memphis, TN, on a hotel balcony in 1968, Dr. King was killed. Thankfully, the movement did not stop. The people Dr. King led picked up his torch and continued the fight. Many who fought alongside him, like Congressman John Lewis and Jesse Jackson, became champions of the struggle.

Nehemiah does not fall for their plot. He receives their message and discerns, "But they thought to do me harm. So, I sent messengers to them, saying, I am doing a great work so that I cannot come down. Why should the work cease while I leave it and go down to you?" Nehemiah has discernment. He recognizes the trap. Nehemiah understands what is happening behind the scene. He cannot stop the work. He cannot be distracted. His presence is too significant.

Nehemiah remains resolute. He doesn't get into petty arguments, defend himself, or get distracted. He knows their request is a distraction that can end badly for him, so he refuses to come down.

To lead well, you must be discerning. You must be wise and pay attention. Traps will be laid, but prayer will serve to warn and guide you. Be careful to talk some and listen more. You have two ears and one mouth for a reason. Listen twice as much as you speak. God will release strategy, ideas, and warnings. Wisdom demands that you pay attention and listen for Her voice.

Sanballat's next strategy involves an attempt to discredit Nehemiah. He sends an open letter to Nehemiah stating,

> It is reported among the nations, and Geshem says, that you and the Jews plan to rebel; therefore, according to these rumors, you are rebuilding the wall, that you may be their king. And you have also appointed prophets to proclaim concerning you at Jerusalem, saying, "There is a king in Judah!" Now, these matters will be reported to the king. So come, therefore, and let us consult together.

Sanballat has one clear intention. He sends the letter without a seal so that the messenger carrying it can read it and share the enclosed information. His letter means to imply that Nehemiah's motives for building are selfish. Sanballat suggests that Nehemiah actually intends to build a dynasty for himself. Sanballat attempts to paint Nehemiah as a blood-thirsty leader who has his eyes on kingship. Ironically, he suggests that he and Nehemiah consult together. Of course, to partner with him would be foolish.

You will likely face similar propositions as you build and grow as a leader. There will be those who are open about their opposition against you. They will try to distract you and oppose what you are doing. If you maintain your resolve, they will seek other strategies. One may be to discredit you as a leader by making incendiary remarks about you, spreading gossip or rumors, or making you afraid. If those strategies are unsuccessful, they may try to tempt you to join them. Don't be distracted and don't be afraid. The enemy of your purpose wants to tempt you to believe that he can stop you, that you aren't called to lead, or that people won't follow you. Ignore the lies of your adversary. Don't get into petty wars. Don't argue. Don't fight. Follow Nehemiah's example. He simply prayed. "Now, therefore, O God, strengthen my hands." You, too, must petition God for assistance. He is the only one who can help you lead despite anything that comes against the work you are building. Petition God with your plans and allow Him to take care of them.

You might think you would be left to build in peace after standing strong, but there is another temptation that every builder will face—the temptation to find some other way to get solutions other than trusting God. Perhaps it may come in the form of horoscopes, burning sage, chakras, or all-out satanic worship. Maybe it will come in the form of making a deal under the table or participating in quid pro quo. No matter how it comes, you must stand strong and resolute. Do not compromise. What God orders, He will always pay for. You can trust Him.

After Nehemiah shakes off the open letter and offer to meet, he goes to the house of a secret informant. The informant suggests that Nehemiah go into the temple and hide since his life is in danger. Shemaiah tells Nehemiah, "Let us meet together in the house of God, within the temple, and let us close the doors of the temple for they are coming to kill you; indeed, at night they will come to kill you." Nehemiah 6:10.

Fear is a deadly adversary. It whispers vile threats to make you worry, get anxious, and move outside of God's timing. Its purpose is to make you listen to its voice and stop.

If Nehemiah obeys his suggestion, he will violate an important commandment from God. Only the priests were allowed in the temple. If he commits this sin, he will compromise his integrity with God and the people he is called to lead. Fortunately, Nehemiah discerns that the man is an informant sent to trick him.

There will be many times when you will be offered compromises. Be careful. Use discernment and ask God for wisdom. God will help you avoid traps that are set up by men to sabotage your success. Set boundaries that keep your integrity intact and stick to them. Boundaries provide safety and prevent the sabotage. They protect the integrity of what you are building.

CHAPTER 7

BE A SOLUTIONIST

Leadership is all about solving problems. You will have to learn to identify problems and develop solutions. Be confident that you can provide answers. Everyone, everywhere has questions. It is your job to help lead them to answers.

There are two main aspects to leadership—competence and followership. An effective leader must not only be skilled; you must also be able to convince people that you are worth following. You have to be believable and you have to establish yourself as a thought leader and an expert.

Sometimes people shy away from the expert adage because they believe an expert has to be perfect or know everything. If that were the case, NO ONE would qualify. In actuality, an expert is actually just someone who knows more than you! Think of it that way and your possibilities become endless.

People follow you when they know you have something of value, and they will pay any price for something that solves the problems that plague them most. Always remember and make it your personal goal to be the best, most competent, and most reliable leader you can be. This is how you will build followers and establish longevity in your field.

Nehemiah was able to accomplish in a few weeks what no one was able to accomplish in years. He possessed an innate ability to see beyond the smoke, the excuses, and the status quo. You must also master this skill. Do not think that because no one has done something, that it cannot be done. Instead, consider that maybe it hasn't been done because YOU haven't done it yet.

Keep your focus on solving problems and building strategies that birth solutions. This really is the winning formula to building influence. God doesn't necessarily choose or use those that are most gifted; He most often uses those who are available. As long as you endeavor to help people, you will never run out of followers, customers, or people who want to be a part of what you are doing.

As you help people heal their pain points, you will gain credibility. Be one who is known for your authenticity and integrity. Be prepared to show provable results and people will look for you. Many people focus all their energy on marketing, but beyond marketing, people want provable results. Never confuse pizazz with legitimate and credible competence. Credibility gives you an authority that will make people want to follow you and submit to your tutelage.

Focus on developing your skill as a leader. Be deliberate about solving problems and you will soon establish yourself as a front-runner, irrespective of your industry. Blossom and become the leader you were intended to be, and the following will come.

In developing strategies, always focus on the value of the work you are doing. Do not fall for the temptation to evaluate your work purely on social media likes and followers. The strongest leaders produce real people with real stories of verifiable results.

Focus on how you have been called to help people. Focus on the work you are doing, not the criticism or applause. Provide and provoke people to be involved in building for themselves. This prevents burnout and garners investment in the end goal. In all that you build, seek to draw the best from others. Put a demand on the gifts inside of them and push them to be the best version of themselves.

You must also master the intricate balance between freedom and responsibility—first for yourself, then for those you lead. Freedom is good, but without boundaries and responsibility, we all get into danger. As a leader, it is your responsibility to equip followers with skills and information so they can flourish. Only those who have solid leadership thrive.

At the end of it all, leadership is about much more than your personal success. It is about guiding people into a life of obedience to their call and purpose. Leadership is preparing people to serve others. As you lead by example, you will build other mature leaders who will transform their culture and world. As they succeed, you will witness the ripple effect of your own impact. You will get to witness the fruit of your labor.

FINAL THOUGHTS

Building influence requires skill and determination. You must have a clearly articulated vision that others may follow. Do not go it alone. Build a team. There is absolutely no way you can do everything by yourself. As you build your team, make sure that everyone is on board with your vision. This task begins with you as the leader. Never lose sight of the fact that everything you do should be adding value to the people you serve. See yourself as a resource that provides services that enhance the lives of others. Your ultimate goal should not be building a dynasty but building people. This is the only way to work toward accomplishing something meaningful. Leaders build people. Leaders create legacy. Leaders replicate themselves in the Earth so that their voice resonates long after they are gone.

Create a community of support and like-minded individuals who will carry the vision and disseminate it. Develop a plan for growth and scale it realistically. Your plan must include partnership with other strong leaders. God has not put everything in any one person. Some have administrative gifts, some leadership, some creative, etc. We need each other in order to sharpen and develop.

As you explore leadership, you will often help someone see themselves in a different light. You are a cultivator of gifts and talents. You help them dig at first, then hand them the shovel to continue the process. People want to be led, but you should also cultivate their unique skills and talents so they can progress on their own.

Gather your team often to develop strategy, remind everyone of the vision, offer support, and provide times of fellowship. It is imperative that you include all members of your team. All parties with vested interest should be encouraged to play a part.

As you grow followers, commit to helping people become the best versions of themselves. Leadership is your opportunity to develop potential and help someone else fly. Do not take advantage of people or try to make them servants or totally dependent on you. Encourage growth and development. This is real impact; This is how you change the world—one person at a time.

When we, as leaders, are clear and concise, it becomes easier for everyone else to do their part. We provide the foundation and encouragement for others to build and grow. In Chapter eight of Nehemiah, Ezra reads the law. Reading the law reminds the people of what they are bound to, what they need to do, and what will happen as a result. Similarly, as a leader, you should regularly revisit your vision and purpose and state it often. Make it so clear that no one is confused about your what and your why. Everyone on your team should understand why you are building. That revelation must begin with you. Revisit your plan and goals and establish new ones as you check off the list.

Avoid mixture, observe kingdom principles for business and honor and acknowledge God as the source. Prayer and fasting are also central components to the success of building.

Whatever you do, do not stop. You must be committed to the vision and what you are called to carry. Minimize distractions. Write the vision. Make it plain. Remain resolute. Establish systems and processes. Ultimately, focus on becoming a leader that you would follow. Then, as you build it, they will come.

CONCLUSION

I've heard it said that leaders are born, not created. I actually think both are true. Some people just have it. Then some have potential, but they need someone to help them draw it out. That is the true essence of leadership—a unique magnetism that draws and connects people. These leaders are the people who always seem to know exactly what to say in any given situation. They are the people who possess the ability to see good in everyone. They help people expand their view of themselves. They are also the ones that everyone looks to whenever a tough decision must be made.

People spend thousands of dollars attempting to buy or build something that really only comes from God. Some are called to lead. Others are called to follow. Discerning which category is yours can save years of heartache and frustration and set you on a path of discovery.

It is of no consequence that you wish to lead or wish to follow. That is not the real issue. There are those who lead and those who are led. If you're not sure which category you fall into, look around. Are there people who are listening to what you have to say? Is anyone following the model you have built and created for your life? That is the real question. You can work on a business plan. You can work on strategy.

You can imagine yourself having the influence that shifts systems and processes on a global scale. But ultimately, whether people will follow hinges on one basic issue, your ability to make people better. If you will meditate on the strategies presented here, develop your personal skill and competence, and keep people development as your primary goal, you will never lack followers. People will naturally be drawn to you. You will build a legacy that is remembered for the value you brought to every life you touch and you will always be viewed as a resource. Then, you can look with confidence and be proud of "Who's Following You."

Do you feel stuck?

Can't seem to figure out your next move?

Allow Me to Help You Unlock your Destiny!

Visit **adriennemayfield.com** and sign up for your personalized transition coaching session today.

www.ingramcontent.com/pod-product-compliance
Lightning Source LLC
LaVergne TN
LVHW010835120826
845149LV00016B/2749

* 9 7 8 0 9 9 9 7 6 9 4 7 8 *